# ...And Baby Makes Two

an adoption tale

by Nanci Christopher

A Samuel French Acting Edition

New York Hollywood London Toronto

SAMUELFRENCH.COM

Copyright © 2009 by Nanci Christopher
Cover graphic design by Greg Szimonsz of Szimple Design

*ALL RIGHTS RESERVED*

CAUTION: Professionals and amateurs are hereby warned that *...AND BABY MAKES TWO* is subject to a Licensing Fee. It is fully protected under the copyright laws of the United States of America, the British Commonwealth, including Canada, and all other countries of the Copyright Union. All rights, including professional, amateur, motion picture, recitation, lecturing, public reading, radio broadcasting, television and the rights of translation into foreign languages are strictly reserved. In its present form the play is dedicated to the reading public only.

The amateur live stage performance rights to *...AND BABY MAKES TWO* are controlled exclusively by Samuel French, Inc., and licensing arrangements and performance licenses must be secured well in advance of presentation. PLEASE NOTE that amateur Licensing Fees are set upon application in accordance with your producing circumstances. When applying for a licensing quotation and a performance license please give us the number of performances intended, dates of production, your seating capacity and admission fee. Licensing Fees are payable one week before the opening performance of the play to Samuel French, Inc., at 45 W. 25th Street, New York, NY 10010.

Licensing Fee of the required amount must be paid whether the play is presented for charity or gain and whether or not admission is charged.

Stock licensing fees quoted upon application to Samuel French, Inc.

For all other rights than those stipulated above, apply to: Samuel French, Inc., 45 W. 25th Street, New York, NY 10010.

Particular emphasis is laid on the question of amateur or professional readings, permission and terms for which must be secured in writing from Samuel French, Inc.

Copying from this book in whole or in part is strictly forbidden by law, and the right of performance is not transferable.

Whenever the play is produced the following notice must appear on all programs, printing and advertising for the play: "Produced by special arrangement with Samuel French, Inc."

Due authorship credit must be given on all programs, printing and advertising for the play.

**ISBN 978-0-573-69712-8**

No one shall commit or authorize any act or omission by which the copyright of, or the right to copyright, this play may be impaired.

No one shall make any changes in this play for the purpose of production.

Publication of this play does not imply availability for performance. Both amateurs and professionals considering a production are strongly advised in their own interests to apply to Samuel French, Inc., for written permission before starting rehearsals, advertising, or booking a theatre.

No part of this book may be reproduced, stored in a retrieval system, or transmitted in any form, by any means, now known or yet to be invented, including mechanical, electronic, photocopying, recording, videotaping, or otherwise, without the prior written permission of the publisher.

## MUSIC USE NOTE

Licensees are solely responsible for obtaining formal written permission from copyright owners to use copyrighted music in the performance of this play and are strongly cautioned to do so. If no such permission is obtained by the licensee, then the licensee must use only original music that the licensee owns and controls. Licensees are solely responsible and liable for all music clearances and shall indemnify the copyright owners of the play and their licensing agent, Samuel French, Inc., against any costs, expenses, losses and liabilities arising from the use of music by licensees.

## IMPORTANT BILLING AND CREDIT REQUIREMENTS

All producers of ...*AND BABY MAKES TWO* must give credit to the Author of the Play in all programs distributed in connection with performances of the Play, and in all instances in which the title of the Play appears for the purposes of advertising, publicizing or otherwise exploiting the Play and/or a production. The name of the Author *must* appear on a separate line on which no other name appears, immediately following the title and *must* appear in size of type not less than fifty percent of the size of the title type.

*...AND BABY MAKES TWO – an adoption tale* (then titled B.U.F.A.) had its first reading on April 19, 2006 and a workshop production February 6-21, 2007 both at the Pacific Resident Theatre in Venice, California (Marilyn Fox, Artistic Director). The production was developed and directed by Paul Linke.

The original production of *...AND BABY MAKES TWO – an adoption tale* was a guest production at The Other Space at the Santa Monica Playhouse in Santa Monica, California. It ran from October 12-November 18, 2007, with a three week extension through December 18, 2007.

The production was developed and directed by Paul Linke and co-produced by Racquel Lehrman of Theatre Planners.

Set Design was by Laura Fine Hawkes, Lighting Design was by Jeremy Pivnick, Sound Design was by Robert Arturo Ramirez, Costume Design was by Jacklynn Evans.

Graphic Design was by Szimple Design, Photography was by Ed Krieger and Casey Neidorf.

The Production Stage Manager was Angelica Estevez.

Voiceovers (in order of appearance):

>	Dick Bell.............................Kevin Kilner
>	Dad.................................Murray Neidorf
>	Rabbi....................Rabbi Jonathan Klein

For more information, video clips and press visit the
*...AND BABY MAKES TWO – an adoption tale* website:
www.andbabymakestwo-anadoptiontale.com

## THE CHARACTER

**NANCI** – 30-50. She is independent by nature with a deep desire to experience motherhood. She is funny, irreverent and quite comfortable with herself.

## THE SETTING

The entire action of the play takes place in Nanci's English garden at the front of her house. There is a brick walkway leading up to the porch where a country style rocking chair sits.

## THE TIME

It is spring...present time.

## ACKNOWLEDGEMENTS

This play would not be what it is without the brilliant guidance and talent of Paul Linke (thank you Mary Lou Belli for introducing us!). As Paul always told me, "Less is more. Just tell your story, Nanci. It is compelling enough to hold its own."

So that is my only "advice"...tell the story simply, connect to the audience whenever you can in an improvised moment and most of all have fun.

I am especially grateful to my friends and family for all their love, support and patience throughout the birth of this "baby" of mine.

Most importantly, I am indebted and blessed by the presence of my real baby and light of my life, Joshua Brandon Neidorf, now almost ten years old...and to Elizabeth Sample Zufelt, his birth mother, who trusted me to raise him.

–N.C.

*For*

*Joshua & Elizabeth*

*With Love*

## JOSHUA'S PRE-SHOW WELCOME

Hi Everybody and welcome to my mommy's show which, by the way, is totally interrupting my life. So anyways, I need you to do a couple of things for me before she starts. First, find the exit door just in case of an emergency. Then be sure to turn off your pagers and cell phones. Also, unwrap any candy you might want to eat now. Please, please do these things, because if you make any noise during the show, my mommy might just turn into "psycho mommy" and I can tell you from experience it's not a pretty sight.

That's it…so enjoy the show! Oh, one last thing. If you have any candy leftover, especially chocolate, you can give it to my mom for me…I LOVE CANDY!

*(Music plays. As the music fades and a growing wind approaches the lights come up on* **NANCI** *standing upstage left. She is in a dripping wet yellow rain slicker [with a hood, of course].)*

*(Slide/Film/News Report of Charleston, South Carolina, September 13, 1999 as Hurricane Floyd's imminent arrival and frenzy are in full swing.)*

**NANCI.** I'd never been in a hurricane before. I'm a California native, so earthquakes were my forte. Give me a 4.8 or a 5.5 and I'd just roll over and go back to sleep. Yet, there I was 3,000 miles away from home waiting for the hospital to discharge to me my newly adopted baby.

I was absolutely frantic at the thought of us being stranded in a hotel in the middle of the storm so I immediately began channeling the overachieving Girl Scout I used to be. Now, just so you know, I earned ALL 44 badges PLUS Sign of the Arrow AND Sign of the Star. I rushed right out to the local Piggly Wiggly. Don't you just love the sound of that…Piggly Wiggly? There used to be a Piggly Wiggly in Encino where I grew up. Anyway, I bought ridiculously huge supplies of baby formula, diapers, wipes, water and canned goods…anything I could get my hands on. I was so prepared for Floyd I could have earned another badge. Then back at the hotel I had a message from the local adoption attorney I was working with.

*(***NANCI** *pushes message button on phone machine.)*

**DICK BELL.** *(voice over)* Nanci, Dick Bell here. This thing is going to hit sooner and harder than we thought. After underestimating Andrew, I am not going to take any chances with Floyd. I know you're supposed to be here for ten days but I want you to get out of Charleston first thing tomorrow morning. After the baby is discharged we'll go straight to the airport. This is an emergency and I will take full responsibility for whatever fallout there may be.

**NANCI.** Twenty-four hours after arriving in Charleston my newborn baby and I were being evacuated! *(sound of thunder)* Welcome to my world...

(**NANCI** *who has already taken her rain slicker off now hangs it on a nearby hook behind the fence upstage left...*)

*(lights change...shift to present time)*

OK, so here's the deal. By the time I hit my mid-thirties my Knight in Shining Armor on a white horse had still not shown up. Shocking, I know. Oh, sure there had been alot of frogs *(low level sounds of many frogs ribetting)*, A LOT of frogs...two in particular even wanted to marry me. I seriously considered one of their offers. *(One frog ribets once.)* There he is. However, at the end of the day, I knew it would have been a disaster of epic proportions. I have always said to friends over the years that if I had married that devoutly committed alcoholic I would surely be divorced and quite possibly be in jail for having killed him. So, I have never regretted that decision. But, clearly, I was faced with quite a dilemma because even though I didn't have the guy to live happily ever after with I still desperately wanted to be a mom.

And believe me, I knew I didn't have any time to waste...I mean, I could literally hear my biological clock screaming. So, I decided to look into all the baby options available.

I investigated everything like an over zealous TV detective; artificial insemination via sperm banks, Chinese baby girls, Russian orphans and domestic adoption through private attorneys. I even asked my best friend, Peter, if he'd give me some of his sperm...twice. He said no...twice.

**NANCI.** *(cont.)* Let me point out here that I was well aware of how fortunate and privileged I was to even be able to consider any of these options. For most people, single or married, the financial cost alone was prohibitive. I was also extremely lucky to be of a generation where adopting a baby as a single woman was allowed and accepted. Not too long ago it had been unthinkable.

I spent two years ruminating over my choices. As for artificial insemination, I decided that I didn't want to create a child and be pregnant by myself. For some women it made a lot of sense but for me it just didn't feel right…mostly because there was this little issue of debilitating mental illness in my family and mental illness is hereditary…which meant swimming around in my gene pool like blood thirsty sharks (think JAWS) were things like severe bi-polar disease, borderline personality disorder, suicide, nervous breakdowns and serious clinical depressions…all the really fun stuff. The thought of passing that legacy on to an innocent child terrified me. I was much more willing to gamble on someone else's genetics than my own.

Oh, don't get me wrong; I wasn't perfect. I certainly was no Betty Crocker. I definitely had "issues" of my own. Ask anyone who has known me for a long time. I was a body obsessed scale-hopping addict among many, many other neurotic things. But after almost twenty years, and yes that's all it took, of intense psychoanalysis and psychotherapy (and OK eventually a little Prozac) I finally felt stable and sane enough to take on motherhood. I just knew there were so many babies in the world that needed a mommy…that needed someone exactly like *me*…a mommy in the making full of love and nurturing to give.

As far as international adoption was concerned, the problem for me personally was that the babies you get are older…usually between nine months to two years old. My thinking was that this would probably be my only child. So, I wanted to have a newborn and experience motherhood to its fullest from the get-go. To have that, private domestic adoption was the only way to go.

My father was not as convinced as I was.

**DAD.** *(voice over)* "Nanci, *I* can find you the sperm."

**NANCI.** "Dad, I am thirty-seven years old. I know where to find it. Actually, I've been finding it for about twenty years now. Come on, you have got to know that sperm is not the problem here."

**DAD.** *(voice over)* "Nance, I am not talking about just any old sperm. I am talking about top of the line Jewish lawyer's sperm, the cream of the crop. Then the child is biologically yours and mine." *(beat)* I am not making this up.

**NANCI.** "Dad, have you really thought about this? I mean, are you seriously going to go to Loeb & Loeb or O'Melveny and Meyers knocking on doors with a little specimen cup in your hand soliciting contributions? Hi, Murray Neidorf. I have a little favor to ask of you. It will only take a minute of your time, I promise. I need some sperm for my single, never-been-married-before daughter. Can you give me a hand? Are you insane?! Look, Dad, I love you, but I don't care about the baby's biology. My mind is made up, OK?"

**DAD.** *(voice over)* "OK, Nance. Whatever you think is best. Lenore, she won't budge an inch."

**NANCI.** So, I began my journey. I hired David Radis, a private adoption attorney, *the* "go to guy" in Los Angeles. David outlined the various things that I could do to find the baby girl of my dreams.

*(A slide of a resume and pictures appear behind* **NANCI**...*)*

I started by writing a three-page personal history with pictures of myself, my family, even my cat, Cleo.

*(A slide of all of Nanci's ads appears behind her...)*

Next, I placed ads in various newspapers across the country. David also had ads in the Yellow Pages with an 800 number in these same cities.

**NANCI.** *(cont.)* Before you knew it I began getting calls. There was Karen from Kansas offering to be a surrogate even though I didn't advertise for one. I was a little puzzled by that at first but thought that it was awfully nice of her to offer. There was Christy in Milwaukee who was not willing to deliver in California or identify the birth father (two of David's deal breakers) and then there was *Kenny* from God knows where with this completely convoluted story. Then another *guy* called from *prison...collect.* Oh, yeah...I was Alice in Wonderland on Mr. Toad's Wild Ride. You can't make this stuff up! Plus there was Cassandra on baby number four, Connie the Liar (there's always a liar) who David caught in like a hundred lies and Leslie from Indiana who was so young and very sweet and just thinking about getting pregnant. I was surprised and disappointed with the results but also equally determined to press on.

A month later David called and I was on my way to Milwaukee to meet Christy who had decided to fully cooperate and was already in the early stages of labor.

I went directly to the hospital and found Christy propped up in bed. "Hi Nanci! Gosh, I'm so glad that you're here. Wait 'til you see him! He's so cute! Oh, I'll get the nurse to bring him in. He's so cute! Oh, I already said that, didn't I?" She seemed a little perky for someone who had just given birth. As I gently picked up this 6lbs. 5oz. blonde, blue-eyed peanut Christy cooed, "The two of you make a good match, don't you think?!" "Yes...yes we do." Hello Austen Beckett...that's in honor of my beloved Grandpa Joe.

The following evening I came back to pick up the baby. Christy asked to speak to me alone, outside, so she could smoke a cigarette. We walked out into the freezing November night. "Listen, Nanci, they're going to release me tonight but keep the baby one more night just as a precaution. *(pause)* You see, the week before the baby was born I smoked a joint. I didn't know that it was laced with cocaine. I never did anything like that before. They said it's just a precaution so don't worry. He's fine. You'll get him tomorrow."

Christy and I arrived at the hospital the next morning as the pediatrician was finishing her examination. "I will not be releasing the baby today, Christy. And if he doesn't stop shaking by tomorrow I'm going to put him on Phenobarbital to wean him off the cocaine. Now why don't you tell me the truth about your drug use." I froze. For the first time I realized the full extent of Christy's lies. She cried, she wrung her hands, she looked pathetic like a deer caught in headlights but she did not budge from her story of one time drug use. A nurse then wheeled the baby over in his bassinette. In that moment I knew that I couldn't... wouldn't be able to keep him. There are people courageous enough to take on drug-addicted babies. I admire and am in awe of those people but I knew that I wasn't one of them. *(to baby)* I'm sorry, little one. I'm so sorry. *(beat)*

Back home I asked Radis what had happened to the baby because I was worried about him. Although David couldn't tell me the details he was able to reassure me that the baby had been released to Christy later in the week and that David had been able to place him with another adoptive family. I was so relieved to know that he was in a loving home...and that he was safe.

*(Soulful country music fades in and then out...)*

"Hi Nanci. This is Marie from Kingsland, Texas. I am 39 years old. I've had eight girls and one boy. This is baby number ten for me. Each of my babies has been with a different father...this guy's name is Jason. Lemme see...he's 6 feet tall, blond and blue-eyed. He's nice, kinda sweet. Just so you know, the only baby I kept was my first one with Lee, my husband at the time. All the others were adopted out. The babies have all been real cute. You can even ask David if you want."

*(airport ambience sounds…)*

**NANCI.** *(cont.)* When we were ready to meet one another face to face I flew Marie and her friend, Ginger, out to LA from Texas for two days. As I waited for her to get off the plane at LAX I looked at every emerging passenger for telltale signs of recognition; a slightly pregnant, petite thirty-nine year old who had lived life on the edge kind of gal with long medium brown hair and sparkling blue-green eyes. Marie did not disappoint. Her persona was every bit as rough around the edges as I'd expected.

However, during the ride to the motel, the brutality of Marie's life revealed itself. "Lee beat me up a lot. I was only seventeen – shit, what did I know. He'd beat me silly and then lock me up for hours at a time in this abandoned garage refrigerator. I could barely breathe. I never knew when he was going to let me out. Man, it was terrifying. Since then, I HATE BEING COOPED UP – can't stand it, not even for a minute." I thought… well, maybe Encino wasn't so bad after all.

Our first stop was at Dr. Matsumoto's office.

*(We hear the sloshing sounds of ultrasound equipment…)*

"Everything looks good, Marie." Then I saw my baby's heartbeat for the first time. I melted and turned to mush. I couldn't believe that this little being growing inside Marie's womb was going to be my child.

We went to see Radis next. "You understand, Marie, that I represent Nanci and not you, that you are entering into this agreement of your own free will." "Oh, yeah, I understand, David. We've done this a few times before, remember?!" We laughed, we hugged, we signed a bunch of papers and we were on our way to Vista del Mar, the agency that was handling my home study, fingerprinting for the Department of Justice and parenting workshops. I also had to submit a detailed personal biography and financial statements. God, it seemed so ironic. Marie could get pregnant by any old guy but I had to jump through hoops to even be *considered* fit to adopt her baby. *(beat)*

Oh, I know, I know, that sounds so judgmental... and, well I admit it, it was. Obviously, I had to get over myself because Marie was my child's birth mother. I wanted to feel good about her and more importantly, I wanted my child to feel good about her, too.

I came to truly believe in my heart that Marie saw having these babies as the one thing in life she was really good at. She knew that she was helping to create families and that she was making a lot of people very happy. I think that it made her feel good about herself, about her place in the world. At the same time she got taken care of for a while where, trust me, in her normal life that was never the case. I actually ended up admiring Marie for at least trying to do something positive with her life in the only way she knew how.

Well, anyway, as soon as the two days were up Marie hightailed it back to Texas and her rural life. I set up phone service for her and started paying all her bills which was the norm.

Three weeks after the amnio test, the results were back – IT WAS A BOY! A HEALTHY NORMAL BOY! Only her second boy! I thought as a single mother I would be better off with a girl because let's face it, I already knew how all the parts worked, but the baby was healthy and that's all that really mattered.

Austen was due at the end of May – just saying that name and thinking of my grandpa made me happy so I decided to give it another chance. I planned for Marie to return to LA on May first for the month, in case she delivered early, which was a distinct possibility, especially with baby number ten...imagine how fast he could decide to pop out!

*(We hear the sounds of ultrasound equipment...)*

10 am Monday morning, May 4th, we were back in Matsumoto's office. *(The sound stops.)*

"Marie, Austen is a little small for this stage in the pregnancy and there is not enough amniotic fluid in the sac. I want to admit you immediately to the hospital for observation, rest and another ultrasound with an expert. The situation could correct itself in a few days and if not you will have to stay in the hospital until you deliver."

"I AM NOT STAYING COOPED UP IN THAT GOD DAMN HOSPITAL FOR THREE WEEKS!"

A couple of hours and a couple of Marlboros later we were settling in at St. John's Hospital.

"Marie, why don't you tell me a little more about Jason."

"I don't know. He's real sweet…but not too smart. He's probably about your height. No, I take that back… maybe a bit taller like 5'8. He's got himself some sandy brownish hair, I think, and his eyes are brown, sorta. Ah, Nanci, he's just a regular guy from Texas."

"Marie, you told me that he was 6' tall, blond hair…"

And then BAM…that's when I got it…MARKETING… *no wonder* she never wanted me to meet Jason!

I waited with Marie for the ultrasound expert to arrive. This woman did not show up until 10 pm. By then, the tension was so thick in the room I considered asking her to do a couple of tests on me just for the hell of it. Who knew, maybe I didn't have enough fluid in my sac!

"The baby is small – probably three and a half pounds – and yes, there is not enough fluid in the sac. However, it could all correct itself in a few days…we'll have to wait and see. On the positive side, the baby's heartbeat is strong and steady; he is not in any distress. Should he become distressed, he can always be taken out early where he'll have a better chance of growing outside the womb. He'd be a bit premature that way, but that wouldn't be something to unnecessarily worry about."

Friday May 8th. "Nanci, it's David. I just got a call from Marie. They are going to take the baby out tonight by C-section because her liver is failing. Apparently, right after you left it was determined that if they don't take the baby now Marie could have permanent, serious liver damage. I need you to stay calm and get back to the hospital as soon as possible."

*(hospital ambience sounds…)*

I had not been in an operating room since I had my ears pinned back when I was a kid. In addition to the mental illness bonanza I'd inherited my dad's ears… suffice it to say they weren't pretty on a ten year old little girl. I got teased constantly so I had that fixed right away. Anyway, for some unknown reason I'd always imagined a birthing room as a warm and cozy kind of place with pink and blue bunnies on the walls so I was surprised to see how blindingly bright and unwelcoming it was.

First, I smelled the burning of Marie's skin, then I saw lots of blood (Oh, God I hate the sight of blood – I could NEVER be a doctor…that's why I'm an actor… we only deal with fake blood) and then, literally minutes later, I saw Austen come out of Marie *(newborn crying)* kicking and screaming. I was stunned. C-sections are fast…burn, cut, open and voilà a baby pops out! He made quite a racket. Everyone in the delivery room started to laugh.

At 3lbs. 14oz. Austen was small, but he was MINE. I immediately began doing the body parts count that all new parents do…it's obligatory. *(pause)* Then it hit me rather suddenly. His hands and fingers looked strangely odd. One of his feet looked really weird, deformed even. A sick feeling settled into the pit of my stomach. But, I reminded myself, "Hell, what do you know, Nanci? You've never seen a baby being born before…they must all look a little funny at first. They have to clean him up. Oh, for heaven's sake, you're hallucinating. Everything is fine." I snapped a few more pictures and sat down on a nearby stool until I heard someone say, "It's a girl."

"No, it's not. HE'S A BOY! THE AMNIO SAID A HEALTHY, NORMAL BOY!" I was staring at my son's genitals in a nanosecond searching frantically for his tiny penis, which I *COULD NOT* find. The doctors were still sewing Marie up. Everyone was blissfully ignorant, except me. The nurses bundled up my son. I followed as they rushed him to neonatal intensive care. I passed my parents on the way. They gave me a thumbs up sign. I didn't respond. I just kept chasing after the nurses who had highjacked my baby.

The first thing I saw when I walked into the NICU was an impossibly tiny baby in an incubator to my left. This baby did not look real. It looked like the fake food they put in display windows at Japanese restaurants to show you what the meal would look like. It was freaky. I felt so confused and disoriented…as if someone had just sucker punched me. I then walked over to where my tiny son was and stared at him. I longed to hold him, touch him, comfort him…but I couldn't, because the nurses were busy hooking him up to hundreds of wires and machines all the while talking amongst themselves as if I wasn't even there. "It's a hermaphrodite."

The neonatal specialist arrived at around 11 pm. This guy was as cold as ice. "His head is not right, his ears are hanging too low, his nipples are spread too far apart, he has six fingers on each hand, an improperly formed penis, which will definitely require surgery to correct, and one foot is webbed. Now, this is just what I can see externally. I suspect that much more will show up internally as well…it usually does with this many external anomalies. We will begin testing him tomorrow."

I went to the waiting room to inform my parents. Their voices wafted in and out of my head. And then my dad said, "Well, Nanci, you can't keep him if he's really that sick. You don't want that for your life." I couldn't breathe. The room was spinning. Then, my dad started to cry.

He didn't know what to do. He couldn't fix it…and my dad, he was, still is, a big time fixer. He's a problem solver…that's what he does for a living. But this time he was completely helpless…and we both knew it. So, I kissed him goodbye, hugged my mother and headed home.

I called the hospital in the morning and talked briefly to Marie. "Austen's alright, whatever the fuck that means. It's Saturday so they haven't started testing him yet but they said they would soon."

The testing revealed that my son had a rare genetic syndrome. I've blocked out the name completely but it was something like Walker Smith Jones Syndrome and it only occurred when both parents carried the recessive gene for it. Marie couldn't have possibly known that she was a carrier because each of her babies had been with a different father. In fact, this syndrome was so rare as to occur in only every two to three million cases. Amnio did not test for it at all. I later learned that amnio didn't test for a lot of things. The doctors said that my poor little baby boy was never going to be able to walk or talk or see or hear.

I called Radis because I was terrified.

"Nanci, Marie is devastated by this. You realize that you may not be able to parent Austen. Often times when the baby is born very sick, the birth mother decides to keep the child. Legally she is still the mother. Do you understand what I am saying, Nanci?"

By Monday morning Marie was no longer taking my calls. *(beat)* I never saw Austen again.

On Sunday, May 24, 1998, twenty minutes after Marie took him off his respirator my sweet Austen died.

*(A voiceover of Nanci's rabbi saying kaddish is heard.* **NANCI** *turns upstage while listening to the kaddish.)*

Five months after Austen's death a small gathering of friends and family joined me in saying Kaddish, the Jewish prayer for the dead. I placed a little sign that said "Austen's Tree" at the base of the baby weeping willow tree in my front yard as my rabbi consecrated the land.

I wish I could tell you that honoring Austen like that made everything all better but it didn't. I was still inconsolable. I was angry all the time. I couldn't get over it. I know Marie did her best but I also needed to be there…because in my heart I was Austen's mommy too.

My poor family didn't know how to help me or comfort me. It was awful; they were awful…the whole situation ripped everybody apart. To be honest, if my best friend, Penny, hadn't flown in from Chicago to help me I couldn't have gotten through that day. Pen was, and still is, my lifeline. And thank God for the rest of my friends who lifted me up and supported me during those impossible months.

*(transition music…)*

About the time of the one-year anniversary of Austen's death I met with David.

"OK, so here's the deal. I want you to put me back in the game…slowly. I'm going back to my original plan so only send me birth mothers that know they're carrying a girl. I've had it with the boys David. Only girls. OK? Only girls."

Two months later in mid-August, David called.

"Nanci, I have just given your name to Elizabeth Sample from Tulsa, Oklahoma. According to her last ultrasound she is carrying a girl. She is going to call you today."

I positioned myself at my little kitchen table–notebook, neurotic pink post-its and pen in hand ready to take copious notes.

*(Phone rings...* **NANCI** *takes a deep breath...)*

"Hello."

"Hi, is Nanci there?"

"Yes, this is Nanci."

"Hi, I'm Elizabeth. I am twenty-one years old. I have a three-year-old little girl named Bryanna with the baby's father who I plan to marry before the baby's birth at the end of September. Me and Bryanna will be moving to Charleston, South Carolina at the end of August to join Buster Jr. where he is stationed in the Navy. (Yep, that's the guy's real name...so there's a Buster Sr. out there somewhere). My mother died in a car accident a year and a half ago. My father is still alive. I have a sister and two brothers. Just so you know, I've got myself some liver disease. I've had it since I was a baby. I even had some surgery for it. But don't worry, it's not hereditary. I must have asked the doctors like a thousand times when I was pregnant with Bryanna if she could get it from me. They always said no and Nanci I tell you, my Bryanna's just as healthy as can be. You see, I don't know how it will affect my life. I get sick a lot so, well, another baby is too much for me."

"Do you need any help with anything Elizabeth? Do you need any money?"

"Oh, no, no. I'm fine. I just want to make sure the baby has a good home. That's all I care about."

I liked her.

Elizabeth and I agreed to meet in Charleston on Saturday evening, September 4th, for dinner at a nearby Olive Garden Restaurant. I encouraged her to bring Buster Jr. along as well because I really wanted to meet the guy...one because he was the baby's birth father and two because I didn't know anyone named Buster and I thought that might be fun. However, I distinctly got the feeling that he wouldn't be joining us. I had yet to speak with Junior personally though through Elizabeth I knew that he was on board for the adoption and willing to sign all the necessary papers.

Elizabeth was about my height (5'6"). She had beautiful thick curly red hair that was shoulder length. Her face was round and covered in freckles. She had full lips and bright blue eyes. She was dressed in a fairly conservative outfit – a pair of beige pants, a crisp white blouse and an embroidered vest that pretty much hid her pregnancy. Bryanna was impeccably dressed in a cute little summer frock, her wispy blonde hair in this half ponytail perched on the top of her head. I used to wear the exact same hairstyle when I was a little girl that my mother called "The Palm Tree." I can't tell you how much this delighted me. Bryanna was so adorable and her huge brown eyes were dancing with excitement…imagine…you're having dinner out at a restaurant, there's a new person and she brought you presents…this was three year-old nirvana! Elizabeth and I were not exactly feeling the same excitement or nirvana. For us this meeting was another test in the ongoing race to the finish line, which was now only three weeks away.

"I'd like to be in the delivery room with you if you don't mind."

"Oh, that would be fine…actually great."

"Good, then let's *plan* on that."

We set up another meeting for the next day, but it never happened. In fact, I couldn't even get hold of Elizabeth leaving me to wonder what the hell was going on. With nothing else to do in Charleston I returned home to LA.

A few days later…I think it was September 8th, Elizabeth called.

"Nanci, I'm sorry I didn't call sooner. I was just so busy

getting things for the apartment, getting all the papers the military needed, taking care of Bryanna and getting married to Buster that I didn't have any time. Plus my liver's been acting up some. Everything's fine now so don't worry."

In the meantime my friend, Donald, and I had made weekend plans to go to San Diego overnight to see our mutual friend, Jordan Baker, in *The Merry Wives of Winsdor* at the Old Globe Theatre. The next thing I knew, the play was over, it was 1:30 am and we were back at this wild motel where two freeways dangerously crisscrossed above our rooms. Now you've only known me for about forty-five minutes but I trust that you know that I did not book this place. I am a five-star girl... four minimum. It is still a mystery to me years later how Donald found this place and why in God's name he booked it! Anyway, there I was standing alone in my room when I suddenly felt compelled to check my phone machine at home.

There were six frantic collect calls from Elizabeth. I rifled through my overnight bag searching for the little black book with all her phone numbers. I called her and Buster's apartment. No answer. I called the hospital next.

"Yes, we have an Elizabeth Sample."

"Well, I'm the adoptive mother for her baby. Where exactly is she?"

"Oh, why she's in Labor and Delivery."

"Ah, could I please speak to her?"

"Sure, I'll transfer you."

"Hi...oh, Nurse Kathy, hi...how's Elizabeth? Oh, I see...you're waiting for the epidural...uh huh... wow, she's dilated to 8 cm already, that sounds good I think...uh oh, uh oh, uh oh, the baby will be here in about an hour or two? No, no, no. I'm not on my way yet. I'm in San Diego. Oh, HOLY SHIT...sorry Nurse Kathy. Let me think for a second here. OK, so here's the deal. I *definitely* won't be there in time for the birth but I will arrive today at some point."

Within ten minutes, Donald and I were packed, dressed and checked out of the motel. *(We hear the sound of race cars speeding around a track.)* Donald was driving like a NASCAR driver just let out of a mental institution.

In the hour it took us to reach the 405 I booked my plane, hotel and rental car. Then I called the hospital again.

"Hi, Elizabeth. It's Nanci. I'm on my way. I'll arrive around 7 pm and come straight to the hospital. How are you doing? What's happening with the baby?"

"Ooh, I'm fine now but there wasn't enough time for the epidural."

"Oh, I'm sorry to hear that. *(beat)* Hello, Elizabeth. Elizabeth…?" Oh, SHIT!

It took me thirty minutes to be able to re-connect. Thirty minutes I didn't know what the hell was going on!

"Elizabeth, I'm so sorry we got cut off…these stupid cell phones! What's going on? What did you mean you didn't have time for the epidural?"

"Well, the damn doctor got here too late and said that I couldn't have the epidural because the baby was coming too fast. Let me tell you Nanci, that was the WORST pain I have EVER had in my whole entire life!"

"Are you alright now?"

"Oh, yeah. I'm just fine. Oh, by the way, it's a boy. Is that alright?"

My knees began shaking. My entire body began trembling. I was so scared. I could not have possibly heard her correctly. Oh, please dear GOD, not another sick baby boy.

"Why, yes, of course. A boy is fine. Is he healthy? 10 fingers, 10 toes, wee wee in the right place?"

*(Elizabeth laughs.)*

"Oh, yes. He's perfect. He came out screaming and hungry. Looks just like Buster Jr. I am never going to forgive him though for not waitin' for that epidural!"

"Oh, I'll be sure to tell him when he's older that he owes you an apology."

"Do you want him circumcised?"

"Ah, yeah I do…but let's wait until I get there for all those decisions, OK? Listen, Elizabeth, I have to go now. I'll see you later today…good job…no I didn't mean to say that…what I meant to say was thank you, Elizabeth…THANK YOU. Bye."

When I arrived at the Charleston airport I found a phone right away and called the hospital only to find out that Elizabeth had already checked herself out! I assured the nurses that I would be there as soon as was humanly possible. I practically ran to the rental car.

*(**NANCI** looks in the rearview mirror as she adjusts it.)*

Then I made the colossal mistake of looking at myself in the rearview mirror…oh là là. I was such a train wreck! All my make-up was completely washed away. I hadn't slept in almost two days and my clothes were beginning to feel crusty. There was no doubt in my mind that I looked every bit as ravaged as any woman who had just given birth. Well, welcome to "The Club" I thought – the sleepless, crusty, bedraggled motherhood club.

Fifteen hours after calling Elizabeth from San Diego, I walked into Trident Medical Center on Sunday, September 12, 1999. It was 7 pm. I could barely walk a straight line and was shocked that no one tried to stop me and drag me off to rehab or something. They would have been justified.

I got myself to the third floor nursery and boldly walked up to the nurses' station. Three nurses turned around in unison, I kid you not, as if rehearsing for the road company of *Hairspray*.

"You *MUST* be Nanci! Elizabeth has told us all about you. He's beautiful, really a beautiful baby."

"Is he healthy?"

"Oh, yeah. He's healthy all right. He's doing great. We've been holding him off for a feeding so you could feed him. Are you ready to meet your son?" **(NANCI** *nods.)*

*(Slide of Joshua in his bassinette appears…)*

And there he was…this tiny bundle swaddled in his hospital issued blanket with his blue and pink striped hat on surrounded by Teddy Bears. Taped above his head on the bassinette was a piece of paper with his vitals and the letters B.U.F.A./BUFA printed on it. I later found out it meant "Baby Up For Adoption." Who the hell knew you had to have THAT written on your bassinette papers? So much I didn't know.

"Can I hold him now?" **(NANCI** *picks up Joshua and whispers in his ear.)* "Hi there Joshua Brandon. Hi there my sweet baby."

Before I could say another word he opened one of his tiny blue gray eyes and gazed up at me…you know, to check me out. He was only twelve hours old but I swear he *knew* who I was.

"Yes, my sweetheart, it's mommy." I took hold of one of his bitty fingers. "I love you, my little man. I love you."

*(Slide of Nanci and Joshua at the hospital when he was born appears…)*

When Elizabeth showed up we hugged and both went on and on and on about how beautiful and perfect Joshua was.

"Oh, Nanci, I just love his name."

*(Slide of Elizabeth and Joshua from the same evening appears, then one of Elizabeth, Nanci and Joshua...)*

As I took pictures of Elizabeth and Joshua together and the nurses took pictures of the three of us news of Hurricane Floyd's fast approaching arrival (remember from the beginning?) was broadcast every two minutes.

*(sound of rolling, rumbling thunder...)*

It was now 10 pm. I was torn between wanting to connect with Elizabeth and needing to get back to the hotel to pack because I was being evacuated in a matter of hours. We stood facing one another in the hospital parking lot.

"Elizabeth, how can I ever thank you enough for the gift you've given me? I promise to love him with all my heart. I promise."

"It's me who should be thanking you, Nanci. I couldn't have done it without you. I knew you were the one the moment I talked to you."

"You are so brave Elizabeth."

"No, I'm not. Nanci, I know I'm not going to live a long life. I know it. I just want what's best for Joshua."

She smiled. We hugged.

"I'll call you once we're back in LA...I love you, Elizabeth."

Then I watched as she drove away. *(beat)*

On Wednesday, January 24, 2007, earlier this year, at 9:08 pm in Tulsa, Oklahoma, our sweet and gentle Elizabeth died of liver failure. She was 30 years old.

*(***NANCI*** looks up to the heavens.)* "Thank you, Elizabeth. Thank you my sweet angel."

*(sounds of jet taking off...)*

When we arrived at LAX I got off the plane with Joshua snuggled on my chest in his Baby Bjorn, his diaper bag and my purse dangling from one shoulder and his car seat thrown over the other one. I looked like any typical mother of a newborn. I was proud as a peacock.

**NANCI.** *(cont.)* I used to be a competitive figure skater as a kid…trained with the great Frank Carroll, Michelle Kwan's coach…it was my passion. I quit to go to college at UC Berkeley and was off the ice for twenty years. Then I got back on about ten years ago…started competing again and winning all sorts of medals and trophies. I had this choreographer named Grant who used to say to me as we were working on a new program… "Nanci, titties out…I need titties out!" Sorry if I've offended anyone but that's how I felt…proud as a peacock, titties out."

My parents were at the gate waiting for us. Remember when you could do that?! Not anymore. They make my kid take his shoes off – what could he possibly have in his shoes?! I could see that they were excited and nervous at the same time…so was I…but there we all were together as a family, us crazy Neidorfs. Joshua was cool as a cucumber still sleeping. After a couple of minutes my mother couldn't stand it any longer.

"Nanci, let me see him."

"Alright already." You know how mothers and daughters are. No matter how old you get it never changes! *(NANCI peels back the blanket covering Joshua.)*

"Oh, he's so beautiful, Nanci. He's just perfect. Come on, let's get him out of here."

Back at home I planned Joshua's bris, baby naming and dip in the mikvah (the holy water) for his conversion to Judaism. At a small ceremony my rabbi consecrated the land in my front yard. *(NANCI places a little sign, "Joshua's Tree" in front of the baby birch tree.)*

**RABBI.** *(voice over)* In Judaism our Torah represents the Tree of Life. So, in the planting of this beautiful tree we first acknowledge the rooting of the past and then the reaching upwards toward the future.

**NANCI.** I WAS SOMEBODY'S MOMMY. Yes me…Nanci Lynn Neidorf aka Christopher (the actress name) WAS FINALLY SOMEBODY'S MOMMY.

*("Movie star" picture of Joshua as a baby, just out of his bath, appears behind **NANCI**.)*

Eight years have flown by *(**NANCI** snaps her fingers)* since Joshua came into my life. If you're a parent you know exactly what I'm talking about. I consider myself to be the luckiest mama on the planet. He's funny, smart and has a kind, loving heart. As if that weren't enough, and believe me it would have been plenty, Joshua grows his hair the same color that I dye mine…I mean how brilliant is that! Can your kid do that?! I don't think so. That is very special! He has my fair skin and my same freckles that flow over his nose and cheeks. He also happens to be left-handed like me and I used to be the only left-handed person in the family! Come on, what were the chances?!

People frequently ask me, "Was it hard to adopt as a single woman?" For some reason this question always baffles me…maybe because the answer is no…and maybe because I truly believe that one good parent is better than two lousy ones. Whenever I talk with other adoptive parents we all agree, without exception, that we can't imagine raising any other child than the one that found us. And they do miraculously find us.

And this kid makes me laugh. Kenahara, as Grandma Ruth says. I mean really laugh, in that deep, hearty no holds barred way. It's such a gift to laugh everyday. One day when Joshua was about three and a half or four years old I was trying to get him to put on his shoes before we went out. He looked at me and with a very serious face said, "Mommy, I just want to wear my feet today." "OK then, feet it is for today. Let's go." And he touches me with his profound sweetness… literally the other night he said, "Mommy, when I'm without you I'm not complete."

*(**NANCI** leans back on the rocking chair as a lullaby is heard)*

*(A present day picture of Joshua in sunglasses with a toothless grin appears behind **NANCI** as she begins to sing along with the lullaby.)*

*(A silhouette of the weeping willow tree appears upstage right.)*

*(Lights slowly fade to black.)*

Wooden Fencing +7
Diagonal Slats
Wooden Slats
Artificial Grass
Flagstone Pathway
Stone Edge Detail
Mixture: Artificial Silk Plantings
Stone Planter
+0"
+4"
+8"
Audience Seat
0
5'
10'
15'
...AND BABY MAKES TWO
Groundplan
Written/Performed by: Nanci Christopher
Director: Paul Linke
Scale: ¼" = 1'
Set Design: Laura Fine Hawkes

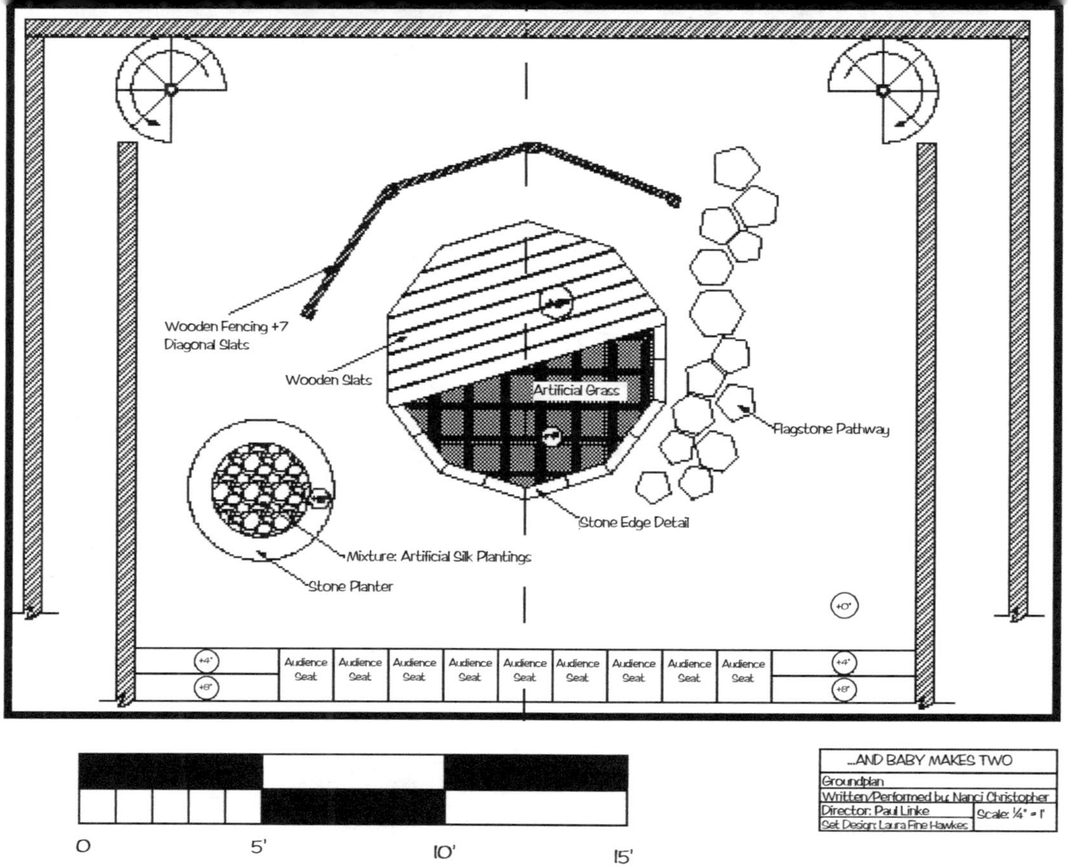

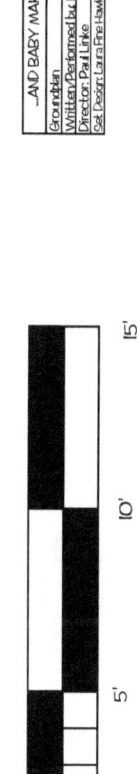